CHILDREN'S

Bedroom Stencils

CHILDREN'S
Bedroom Stencils

Magie M. Maule

Angus&Robertson
An imprint of HarperCollins*Publishers*

For my darling children:

Madeleine-Sophie Walker
Benjamin James Maule
Isabelle Hesiöne Maule-Clark

AN ANGUS & ROBERTSON BOOK
An imprint of HarperCollinsPublishers

First published in Australia in 1992 by
CollinsAngus&Robertson Publishers Pty Limited (ACN 009 913 517)
A division of HarperCollinsPublishers (Australia) Pty Limited
25-31 Ryde Road, Pymble NSW 2073, Australia

HarperCollinsPublishers (New Zealand) Limited
31 View Road, Glenfield, Auckland 10, New Zealand

HarperCollinsPublishers Limited
77-85 Fulham Palace Road, London W6 8JB, United Kingdom

Copyright © Magie M. Maule, 1992

National Library of Australia
Cataloguing-in-Publication data:

Maule, Magie M.

 Children's bedroom stencils.

 ISBN 0 207 17425 3.

 1. Stencil work I. Title.

745.73

Printed in Hong Kong

5 4 3 2 1
96 95 94 93 92

CONTENTS

PREFACE

Such has been the popularity of my first two books — *Australian Stencil Design* and *Australian Stencils for Children's Rooms* — that I seem to have been writing ever since. Here I am prefacing my fourth book, with a fifth book, *Floral Stencils*, half finished.

In *Children's Bedroom Stencils* I have included more general and more European animals and motifs, as well as several designs we couldn't quite fit into the previous books. Within these 150 designs you will find traditional motifs, with a bit of humour thrown in as well. Use these stencils for tiny babies and toddlers, for teens and in-betweens.

To my great joy my younger daughter Isabelle has contributed some of her wonderful animals — pigs are obviously in this year. She seems to be following in mother's footsteps.

I do hope you find this book inspiring and entertaining, and get as much fun out of using these stencils as I have had in designing them.

Magie M. Maule

INTRODUCTION

FIRST THINGS FIRST

Stencilling is one of the most popular and economical forms of home decoration. Part of the renewed interest in this ancient form links to an appreciation of the work of the artisan, of the homemade as opposed to the manufactured. Besides, stencilling is an easy skill to pursue, and it provides instant results. With a little patience, and following instructions carefully, the artistic amateur will achieve delightful results.

A stencil can be made from cardboard, plastic, or even metal, into which you cut holes to form a design. Paint is brushed or sprayed through these holes and onto your surface to create the pattern. The pieces of stencil holding the holes together are called bridges or ties; they are important in outlining or highlighting sections of the design, and they are arranged to make the stencil strong.

Stencilling is an economical and efficient art form, as you can use one stencil to make many repeats of a design. For the small amount of initial effort required in cutting your stencil you are rewarded by being able to decorate large areas very quickly.

Read these instructions very carefully before you begin stencilling. The stencils in this book simply require that you photocopy your chosen design, trace it onto a stencil board, cut out all the black areas and brush or spray paint through the holes you make — this is where your colour will appear.

Most of the designs in this book are stencilled in one colour. If you would like to use more than one colour, instructions are provided in the pages to come.

Some of these stencils are very simple, others will take a bit longer to cut out. I think you will agree that these more complex designs are well worth the effort.

Make sure your stencils are large enough to work with easily, and are in good proportion to whatever area you are working on — be it walls, floors, furniture or fabric. Some designs may need to be enlarged using a photocopier or grid.

TRACING YOUR STENCIL
Materials
Carbon paper
Oiled stencil board or acetate sheet*
Sharp pencil or pen

The traditional method for tracing your stencil is to trace the design onto tracing paper from your book, but if you have enlarged your design on a photocopier, you can draw directly around that.

First place your tracing or enlarged photocopy on top of a piece of carbon paper, underneath which is the stencil board or acetate — this makes a three-layer sandwich.

The stencil board should have straight edges and the carbon paper and photocopy be placed at right angles to it and secured with drawing pins to prevent movement.

Next, draw firmly around all the outlines with your pencil. Press firmly down through the carbon paper onto the stencil board or acetate so that you transfer the design via the carbon onto the stencil board.

---

* Acetate is transparent and waterproof and is a good material to use when the stencil is simple or when you have an extensive project, such as stencilling an entire room. It will last throughout your entire project, unlike a weaker material such as cardboard. Despite its advantages, some people do not like to use acetate because it is expensive and because it can be difficult to cut smoothly. You can use acrylic sheet instead of acetate. Although acrylic sheet is less transparent than acetate, it is more pliable and so it is easier to cut around corners.

Make sure that your stencil board is at least five centimetres larger than the design (on all sides) to leave a border to prevent paint accidentally getting onto the background.

CUTTING YOUR STENCIL
Materials
Sharp knife or surgeon's scalpel (always keep it stuck into a cork for safety), or sharp nail scissors (some people find these much easier to use)
Cutting board (I always use the cardboard backs of tracing pads — but you can use a sheet of metal, or a glass plate with the edges covered with sticky tape)
Sticky tape (insulating tape for glass edges)
Needles (to poke out small circles if required)
Fine sandpaper (to sand down projections on the back of the stencil board if you have poked out holes with your needle)
Stencil board with design drawn on it

Place the stencil on the cutting board, holding the knife edge at an angle of 45 degrees as you cut. Cut out all the outlined areas and remove the pieces released. Work from the smallest areas to the largest to prevent weakening the bridges or ties (the thin strips of material that separate the holes and hold the stencil together). Take care with corners. If you overshoot the outlines you might cut through 'bridges'; if you do this, mend this cut with sticky tape on both sides for strength.

Small areas and holes can be poked out with needles, and the rough bits on the back of the stencil caused by this need to be finely sanded back, to keep the stencil flat when printing.

When all the areas to be removed have been cut out, your stencil is finished and ready to print.

APPLYING YOUR STENCIL
PAINT
Always use oil-based paint when painting floors, wood or furniture because it's traditional, and I like the feel of it. Most importantly, the colours are very intense, while acrylic paints tend to be rather wishy-washy (although this is improving).

You can use acrylic or other paints on walls if you like, but I almost always stick to oils as I like to use special finishes with my stencils, which work better with oils. Artists' oil paints are fine, or you can use special stencilling paints if available.

Mix the oil paint with turps in a flat-bottomed container, like an old saucer or plate, until you have a thin cream with no lumps. If you are using more than a quarter of a litre of paint it should be strained through an old stocking to make sure there are no 'bits' in the mixture (particularly if you are using paint from a pot that has been used before) because paint brushes often have dust or grit in them that gets transferred to the container.

BRUSHES
A few different sized stencil brushes may be required depending on the kind of stencilling you are doing.

For general work one fine, two medium and one large brush should be enough. A brush for each colour, all of the same size, is the rule, because you can't wash out the brush till the end of the work (turps in the brush would thin out the next lot of paint and make it smudge the work around the edges). To clean your brushes just wipe them on an old cloth to remove surplus paint. There can be a very small amount of turps on the rag.

You can stencil without a brush by using an air brush or spray can. If you do this you will need to protect the surroundings with larger areas of masking tape and newspaper as spray paint can drift a long way from the paint site. Wear a mask, hat and overalls when spraying.

HOW TO PAINT WITH A STENCIL BRUSH
Stencilling is not like conventional painting where the brush is moved from side to side. A stencil brush is always held like a pen between thumb, index and second fingers, not like a conventional brush. The flat cut-off bristles on a stencil brush are held parallel to the printing surface and the painting motion is one of tapping through the stencil with the loaded

brush, lifting the brush off cleanly each time, but tapping rapidly and making sure that you tap from the edges to the centre of each opening in the stencil to stop paint creeping under the stencil and smudging the print. This tapping motion is called *pouncing*.

Once your paint is mixed you can try out your first stencil on paper. Dip your brush into the paint so that only the tips of the bristles have contact with the paint. Now tap onto a piece of newspaper. Keep tapping in several places until most of the paint is off the brush. When you think there is hardly any paint left on it, you can start *pouncing* (tapping) your brush through the design using as little paint as possible. This ensures that the design has a good crisp edge and that it dries quickly.

STENCILLING ON DIFFERENT SURFACES

As a general rule, before you start stencilling you should prepare the surface you are going to use. Make sure that all surfaces are finely sanded, brushed free of all dust and are free from grease. Holes and faults should be filled a little high and then sanded back flat. Furniture and painted wooden surfaces in good condition can be washed down with sugar soap or detergent. Any slightly irregular or shiny surface should be sanded back with water and 'wet and dry' sandpaper using small circular movements. This produces a matt surface that takes paint easily.

Materials
Oil paint
Stencil brushes (small, medium or large depending on the work involved)
Spray mount and solvent
Chalk, chalk-liners and a plumb bob for walls
Set square
Pencil
Masking tape
Newspaper
Old rags
Old saucer or plate
Turpentine
Sheet of drawing paper
Scissors

WALLS
When stencilling walls, you will probably be stencilling repeating borders, spot designs where motifs are regularly placed but not connected, or a repeating, all-over design. Whichever pattern you are doing, the structure of the design should be mapped out in chalk, which can then be rubbed off easily afterwards.

First use your plumb bob to establish your true uprights (straight vertical lines) by hanging it from the ceiling and letting it swing until it comes to rest. The plumb bob string should be covered with chalk by running your chalk up and down the string until it is well coated. Hold the string of the bob at top and bottom against the wall (you will need two people) then pull out the string in the middle towards you, like plucking a guitar string, and let it flick against the wall — it will leave a perfectly straight chalk line from which you can measure all other vertical and horizontal lines using a set square. Map out the geometric structure that you require for all-over repeats, for example, so that you will know where every stencil will fall in squares, diamonds, bands and so on.

If you are doing a line of stencils you will need to know where to position your second, third, and subsequent stencils in relation to the first. On acrylic this is easy. Place your cut out stencil next to the original design. Decide what space there will be between them and make nicks or large dots at two or three places on the acrylic; when you make the next stencil design, you will always place these dots or nicks in the same spot in relation to the previous print (you will have to wait for the previous stencil to dry, otherwise you will pick up paint on your stencil board).

On stencil board that is *not* transparent, punch out small holes that you can see through, or use nicks in the edge of the stencil, so that you always get the same piece of the previous stencil showing through the hole. This procedure ensures that the repeats are evenly spaced. Try this system on clean paper before you start on the walls.

To stencil walls, stick the stencil to the wall with masking tape (not sticky tape) or spray the

back of the stencil with spray mount, following directions for its use on the back of the can. When you have painted your design through your stencil it must be carefully removed and, for repeats, stuck down again for the next stencil.

If you use spray mount, keep the stencil on a dry, shiny surface to avoid it picking up dust or grit, or if you are using stencil board, keep your stencil on clean newspaper and wipe off any surplus paint now and then to avoid build up. You can clean your stencil properly with turps at the end and store it flat. The spray mount must be removed with its own solvent.

Your stencil work should be protected with a coat of matt, satin or gloss varnish, as desired.

USING MORE THAN ONE COLOUR

By following a few guidelines, stencilling in two or more colours will give beautiful results.

It is important that the stencil be left in place until all colours are applied. When painting each colour, use masking tape to mask off the areas where other colours will appear. The instructions (on facing page) for stencilling the duck motif apply also to the other stencils in this book.

FLOORS

Floors need a little more explanation than walls, but they are easier to deal with than walls or ceilings as you have both hands free. Floors should be sanded smooth — by a professional sander if possible, who will also hammer in all loose nails, and fill in nail head holes and other defects. The floor should be given two good oil-based undercoats after it has been thoroughly vacuumed and gone over with a *tack* rag, which you can buy from a hardwear shop. A *tack* rag is a cloth made sticky with impregnated varnish. It will pick up dust and bits from any surface that you have sanded — it is an *invaluable* piece of equipment.

Each coat of paint will take 24–48 hours to dry, so the room should be locked to avoid cats, dogs and children leaving little traces. Under-coating is followed by two coats, also oil-based, of your chosen background colour. You can buy special fast-drying floor paints that are excellent. You now have a good surface to work on. One last vacuuming and thorough going over with your tack rag and you are ready to stencil.

If you are making a repeating design all over a floor you lay out your work using chalked string the same as for a wall. If you are using a diamond or chequerboard design, two lines taken from the corners and crossing in the middle will give you your centre.

When painting the floor there are two golden rules: i) cover your hair completely as some hairs always drop into the wet paint. (If you find hairs on the floor while it is still wet, you can remove them with sticky tape wrapped around your index finger by using a light dabbing motion); ii) Don't get trapped! Start in the far corner and paint your way out of the room towards the door. If the floor is made of boards, paint along the line of the floor boards. If you are putting down another covering in sections (craftboard for example) these can be undercoated before laying.

When your design is finished and completely dry you will need to varnish it. Five coats of 'Satin Clear Varnish' by Feast & Watson give a good result. Follow the directions on the can and allow the correct drying time. You will now have a hardwearing floor that can be simply mopped clean with a damp sponge. If the surface starts to wear, give it a light sanding and apply a few more coats of varnish.

It is particularly important to strain paint and varnish as the cans *always* end up with bits of dirt and grit in them; they are transferred from the floor to the brush no matter how carefully you have cleaned and dusted the floor.

FURNITURE

Furniture should be in sound condition, so repair where necessary. Fill all holes and sand with 'wet and dry', whether it is painted or clean wood, till the piece is smooth all over. Prep-aration is the most important part of a well-painted piece of furniture.

Use two oil-based coats of undercoat and two *thin* coats of the chosen main colour. Use paint

DUCK MOTIF

This step-by-step stencil of ducks indicates how separate colours build up into a complete design.

If you want to use different colours on the one stencil, identify the areas that will appear in each colour. Some of the stencil designs in this book have been printed in different shades of grey as a guide to where different colours can be used.

Work with one colour at a time, masking off any spaces on the stencil that you don't want printed in that particular colour. Once you print the first colour, cover all those spaces on the stencil with masking tape and print your next colour, and so on for each new colour. Small lines such as facial features or other details will need to be painted separately by hand.

Sometimes you can take a short cut and produce a third colour when painting with two. If you stencil two colours, say yellow and red, any area where they overlap will print orange.

Don't remove the stencil until you have finished all colours.

thinly, otherwise you will get dribbles. If the worst happens and you do get a paint dribble, remove it carefully with a scalpel when dry and sand smooth. Using water, sand lightly in-between the colour coats with fine 'wet and dry' using a circular motion. Clean off the 'mud' that appears during the process with hot soapy water and dry thoroughly. When quite dry you can begin stencilling. Choose your stencil design to suit the style of the piece of furniture and make sure it is in good proportion to the size of the surface on which you are working — neither too large nor too small.

Once your stencilling is dry — up to 48 hours — protect it with several coats of satin or gloss varnish, whichever is appropriate to the appearance of the piece. I recommend between three and five coats, lightly sanded with 'wet and dry' between coats. This will ensure you end up with a piece of furniture silky smooth to the touch, which can be further protected with wax polish.

FABRIC

Stencilling on fabric is essentially the same as for the surfaces already described, but there are a few differences, as you will see.

Materials

Clean newspaper, obtainable from your butcher (not newsprint — old newsprint can leave dirty marks)
Fabric dyes or paints
Stencil brushes
Drawing board or flat printing table
Drawing pins
Fabric
Metallic spray

If you are using stencil board you will have to waterproof your stencil by giving it several coats of metallic spray paint on both sides, because fabric dyes and paints are water soluble and will make the board disintegrate. If you use an acrylic or plastic stencil it will already be waterproof.

STENCILLING BORDERS

You can make any motif in this book into an interesting border by repeating it at regular intervals or by repeating combinations of designs. To link this border and make it more attractive, place a continuous line above and below it. An ordinary stencil will not make such a line, so follow this procedure.

Mark a straight line where required using the chalked string method. Place a piece of masking tape of the desired width (use 2 or 3 pieces if you require a wide band) around the entire room on this chalk line. The tape is your 'stencilling band'. Use coloured tape to avoid confusion. Next take masking tape

(about 2.5 centimetres wide) and place it both above and below your stencilling band. Do this around the entire room. Now you have a band of wall to be stencilled in the usual way.

When using tape, tack it off against the carpet or your clothes as you work — this will remove some of the stickiness. This way you avoid the risk of removing parts of the wall or paint when you remove the tape.

Be warned that it is impossible to get a neat continuous band in any other way. Don't try any inventive short cuts: they've all been tried before!

New fabric should be washed to remove any dressing and then ironed and pinned out flat. Fabric or garments should be pinned or taped firmly to a hard, flat surface on top of several layers of newspaper to absorb excess dye or paint and to reduce blotching. Remember to put paper *inside* garments as well, otherwise you will have two printed layers — front and back!

Stencil with your brush exactly as for the oil paint method and leave to dry. Treat according to the instructions on the fabric paint. After stencilling, lampshades, curtains and blinds can be sprayed with 'Scotchguard' waterproofer to protect them.

You might also like to stencil a design onto tapestry canvas and embroider as usual. This way you can begin to create entire room schemes.

PAPER

There are so many things you can make out of stencils on paper — lampshades, book covers, drawer liner. Try stencilling on some of the lovely rag papers available, or vellum or Japanese handmade papers. Try making your own wallpaper by printing on rolls of lining paper.

Materials

Stencil brushes
Artists' watercolours or gouache colours, poster colours, inks etc.
Any kind of absorbent paper, parchment, vellum etc.
Metallic spray paint

For this stencilling use the brush as for previous methods, or use matt paint from a can, or ink using a mouth spray.

First of all waterproof your stencil by spraying both sides of it with several layers of metallic spray paint and leave to dry. Pin out the rolls or sheets of paper, or tape the extreme edges, padding underneath with newsprint.

Secure your stencils with pins or tape, then stencil in the usual way, holding your brush like a pen and using the pouncing technique described earlier, with very little paint on the brush. The work can be protected with a spray of clear varnish especially designed to make paper moisture- and dirt-proof ('Ascro Crystal Clear Varnish' is ideal).

If you want to stencil a lampshade it is best to find some good quality card, parchment or vellum and cut it to shape, stencilling while flat and assembling the shade later. Ready-made lampshades can be stencilled with spray paint, using plenty of masking tape, or with coloured ink and an artists' mouth spray, again masking surrounding areas well. Protect your design with clear paper varnish and it will wipe clean. You can also make lampshades without paint by cutting the shade out like a large stencil and lining it inside with different coloured paper or cloth. This gives an interesting effect when the light shines through.

Stencilling has endless possibilities and with this skill you will be able to transform your children's rooms, making them artistic and unique in a world of mass-produced products. There is real scope for creativity and playing with this interesting form, altering designs and combinations to suit yourself — and it will all be your own handiwork.

Happy stencilling!

FURTHER READING

Maule, M. *Australian Stencil Designs for Children's Rooms* Sydney, Angus & Robertson, 1990.

Maule, M. *Decorative Stencils for Interior Design* Sydney, Angus & Robertson, 1991.

McCorquodale, J. *History of Interior Decoration* Oxford, Phaedon Press, 1983.

de Dampierre, F. *The Best of Painted Furniture* London, Weidenfeld and Nicolson, 1987.

Waring, J. *Early American Stencils* London, Dover Press, 1968.

BERRIES, BOWS
AND BORDERS

23

AT THE CIRCUS

Hand paint the elephant's eye.

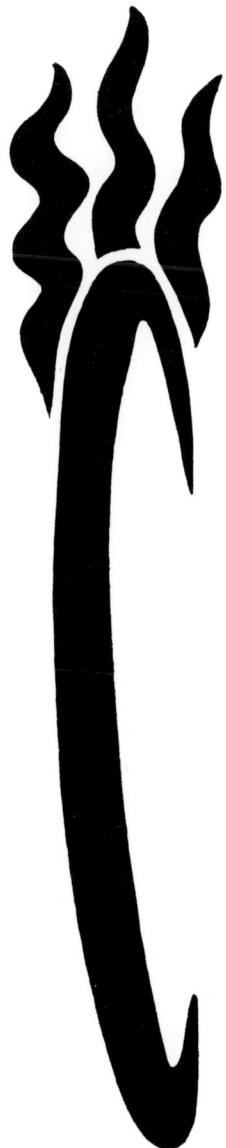

Add an eye in by hand.

Give the pig his buttons and facial features by hand.

Paint an eye on the echidna by hand.

Add an eye to this sporty little dog by hand.

Use your imagination and paint
a face onto this clown.

Add an eye to this clown by hand.

Add whiskers and an eye to the seal.

Paint in eyes and buttons by hand.

FARMYARD CHARACTERS

*Paint facial features by hand
onto all these cows.*

Give these animals character by adding facial features by hand.

Give the lamb an eye.

Add in an eye by hand.

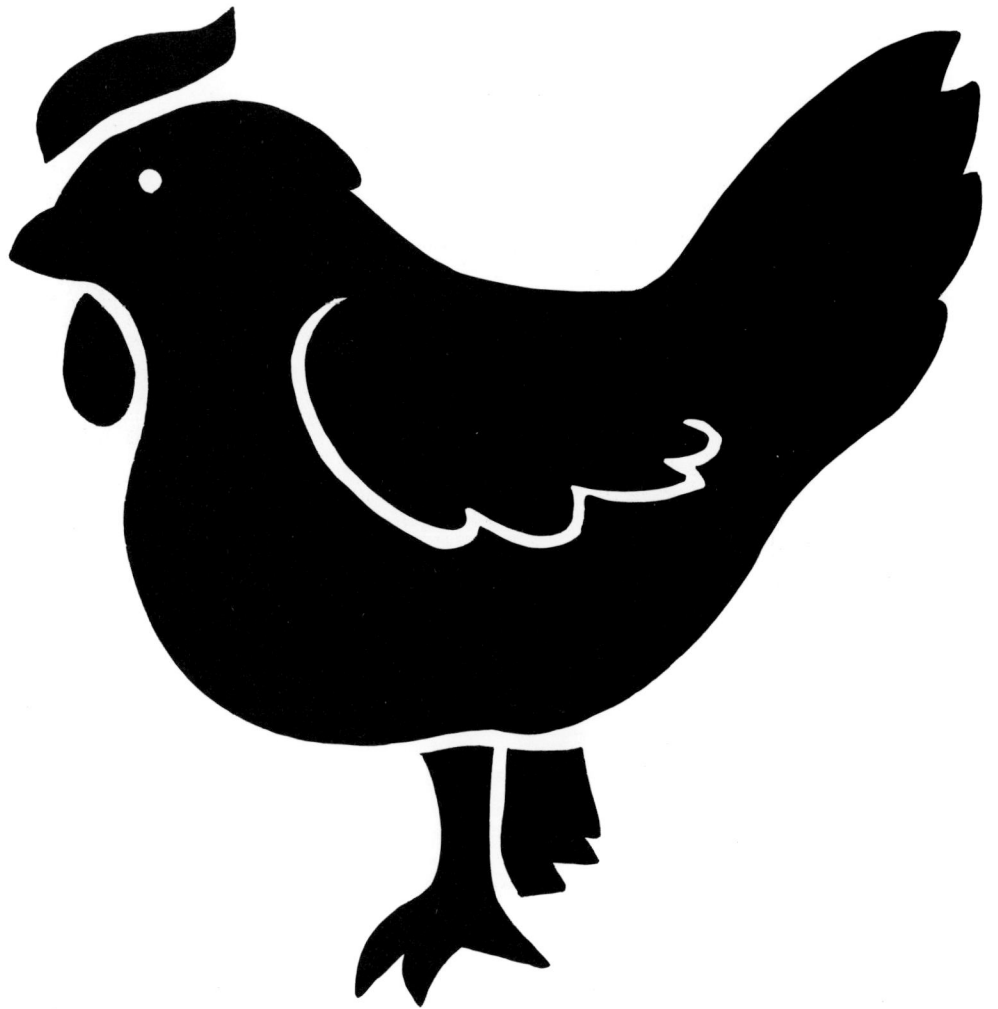

Paint eyes and wings on the poultry.

Paint in facial features by hand.

*Paint eyes and wings on to these
birds by hand.*

48

Add eyes by hand.

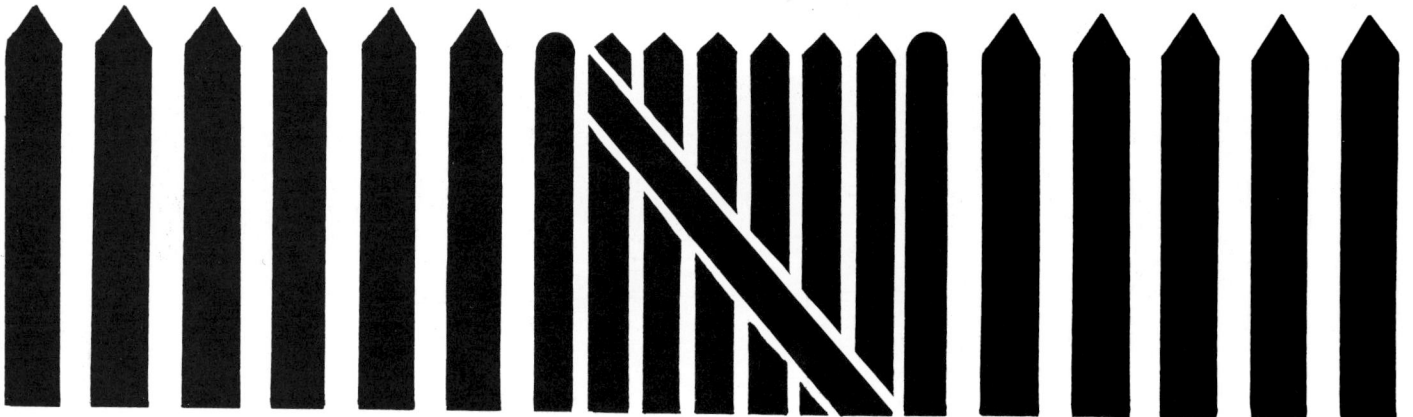

DINOSAURS AND DREADFUL BEASTIES

Give these dinosaurs eyes.

52

Paint eyes on this frill-necked lizard.

Give these dinosaurs eyes.

Hand paint eyes.

Hand paint eyes.

Add facial features to these reptiles by hand.

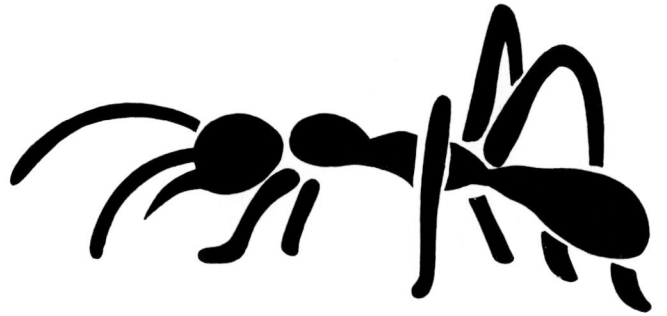

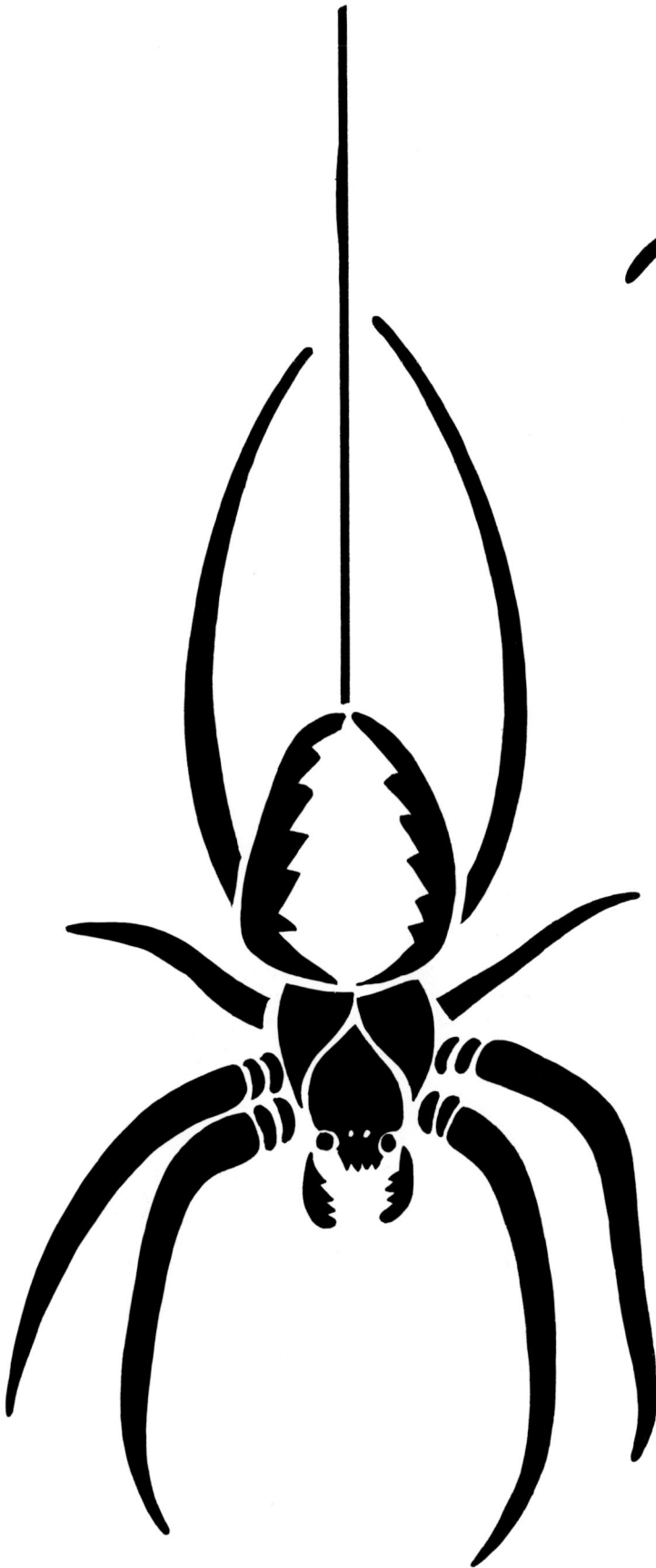

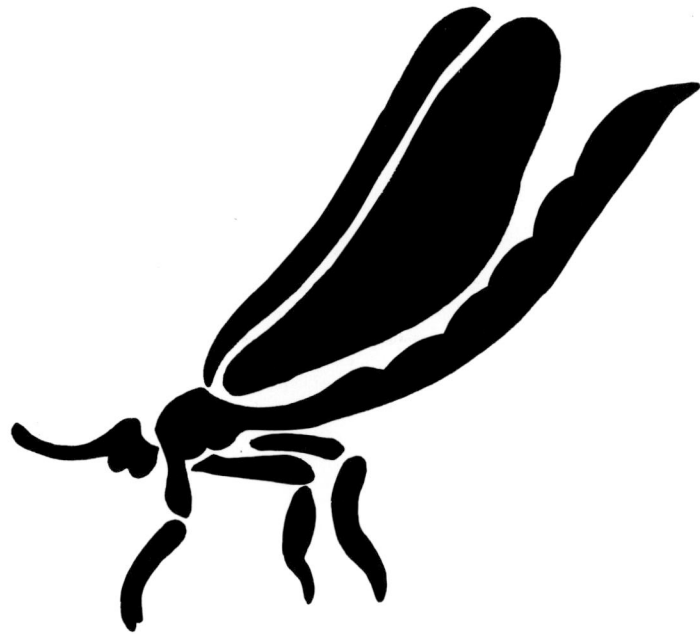

Add details to the head of this spider.

Paint an eye onto this sabre-tooth tiger.

MOUSE TALES

Paint in eyes and whiskers.

Give the skating mouse an eye.

Paint in eyes.

70

Paint in eyes and whiskers.

ANIMALS FROM ALL OVER

Paint eyes on the rabbits.

Paint in eyes.

Hand paint eyes.

Paint in eyes by hand.

Paint in eyes, and the tail of the bear cub.

ISABELLE'S ANIMALS

Paint facial features in by hand.

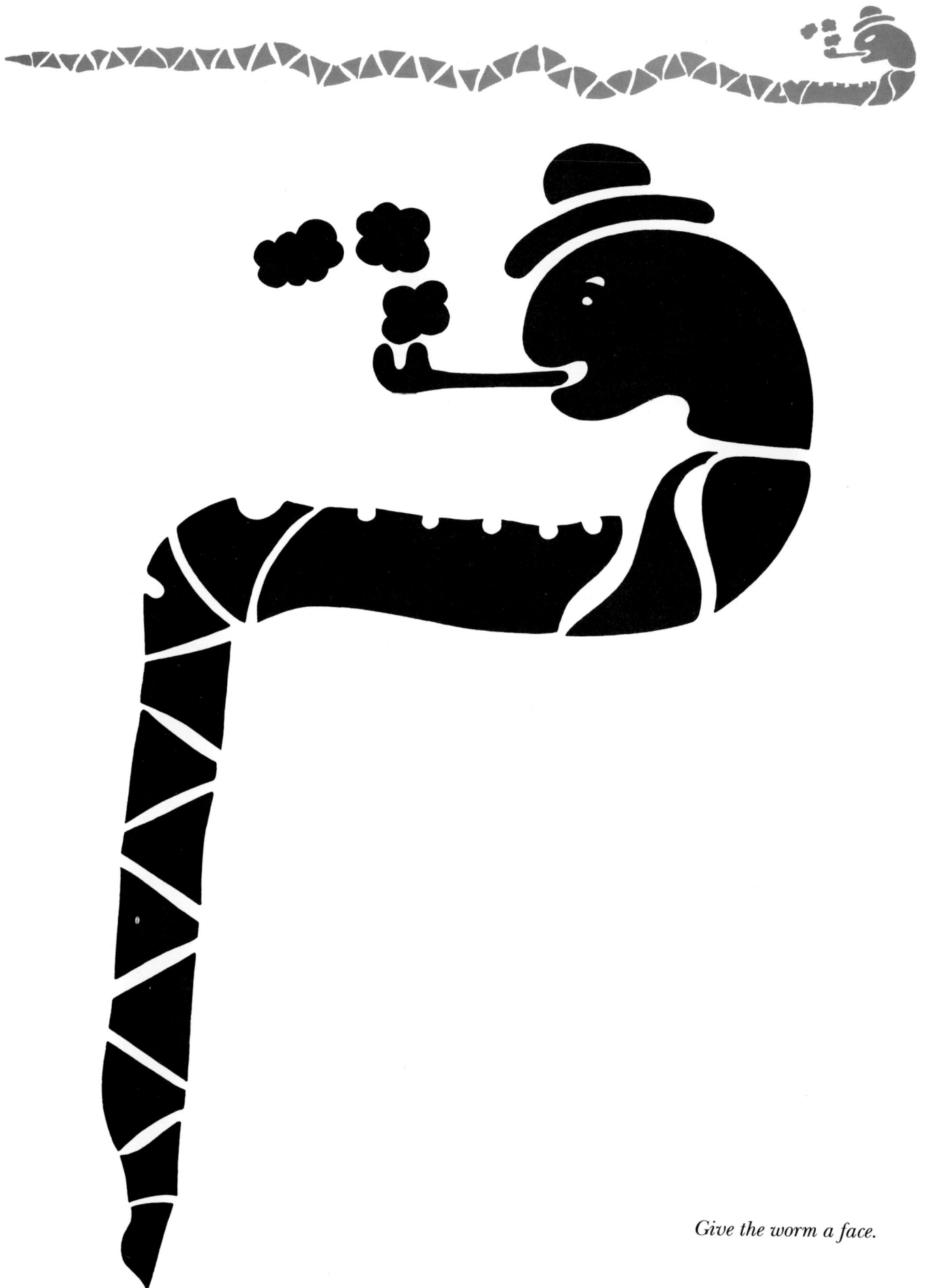

Give the worm a face.

Paint the face on the koala by
hand.

Add facial features by hand.

FLYING THINGS

Paint the eye onto this baby bird.

Finish detailing the stork by hand.

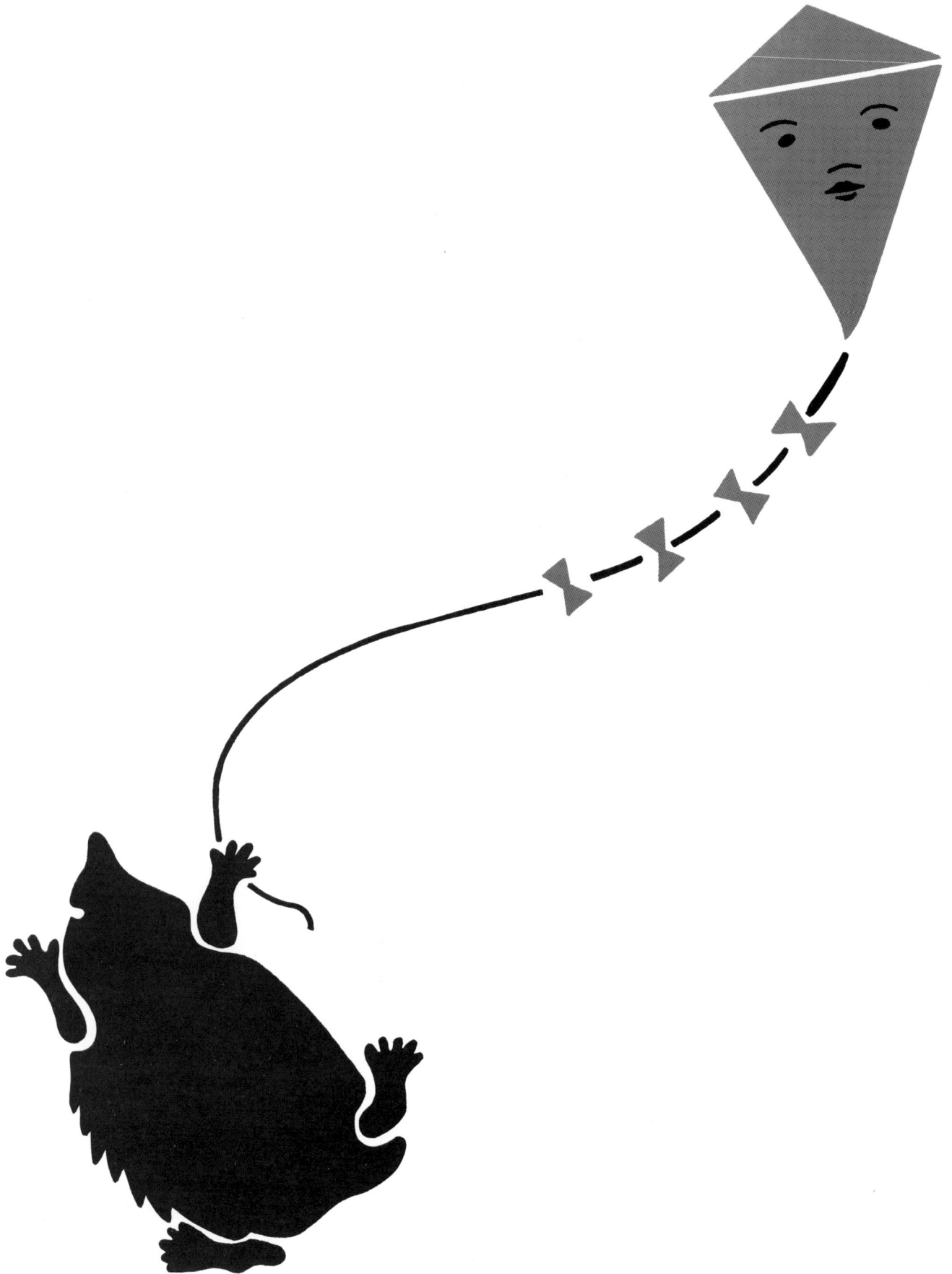

FROM
THE TOYBOX

Paint the eye in by hand.

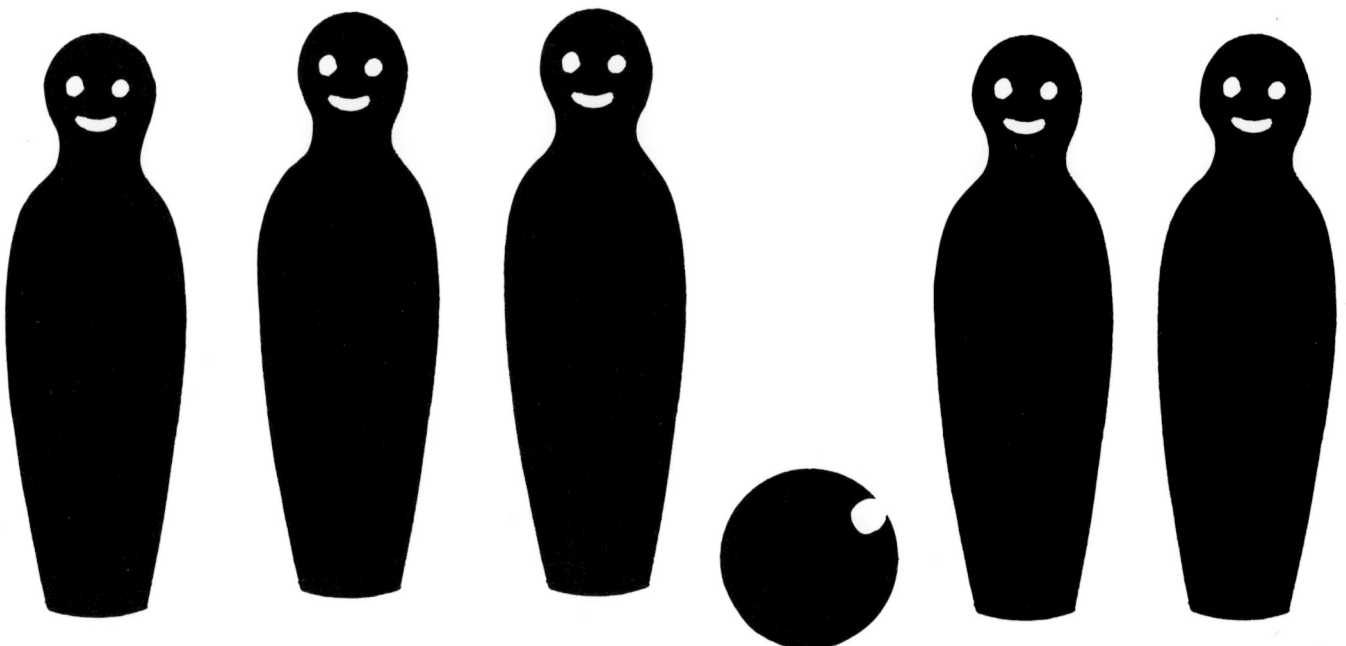

Add faces to these skittles by hand.

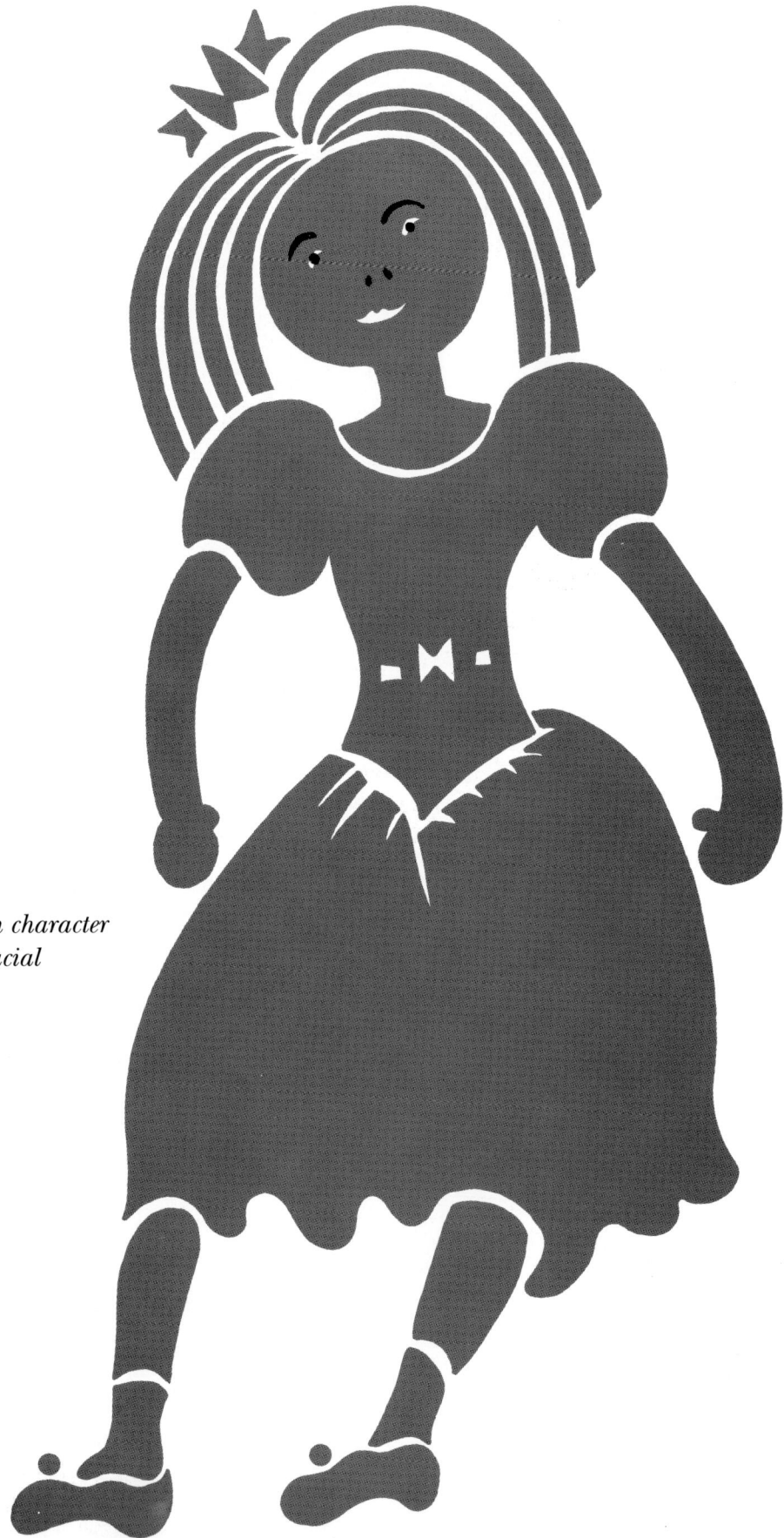

Give this doll her own character as you paint in her facial features.

Paint facial features by hand.

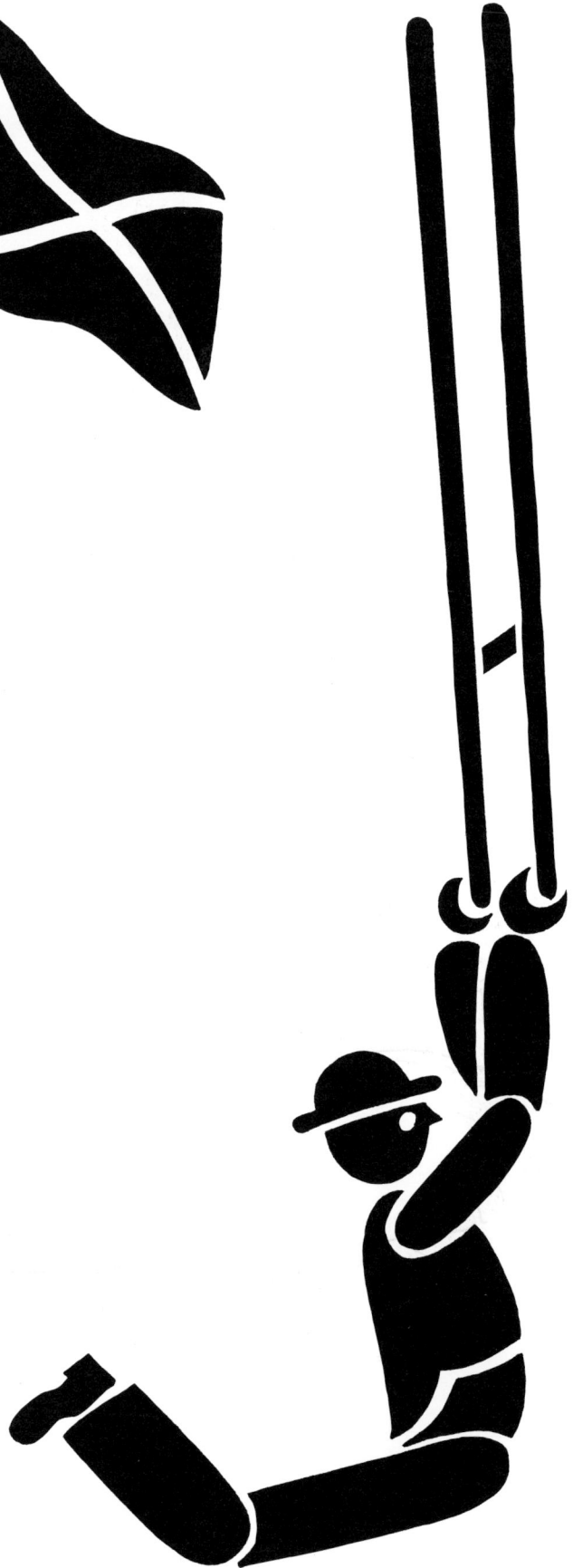

Add facial features to these bears by hand.

ALPHABETS AND NUMBERS

ABC

DEFG

HIJK

ALPHABETS

LMN

OPQ

RST

113

ALPHABETS

ABCD

EFG

HIJK

L M N
O P Q
R S T

116

ALPHABETS

U V W

X Y Z

1 2 3 4

ALPHABETS

A B C D
E F G
H I J K L
M N O P

Q R S

T U V W

X Y Z

1 2 3 5

ALPHABETS

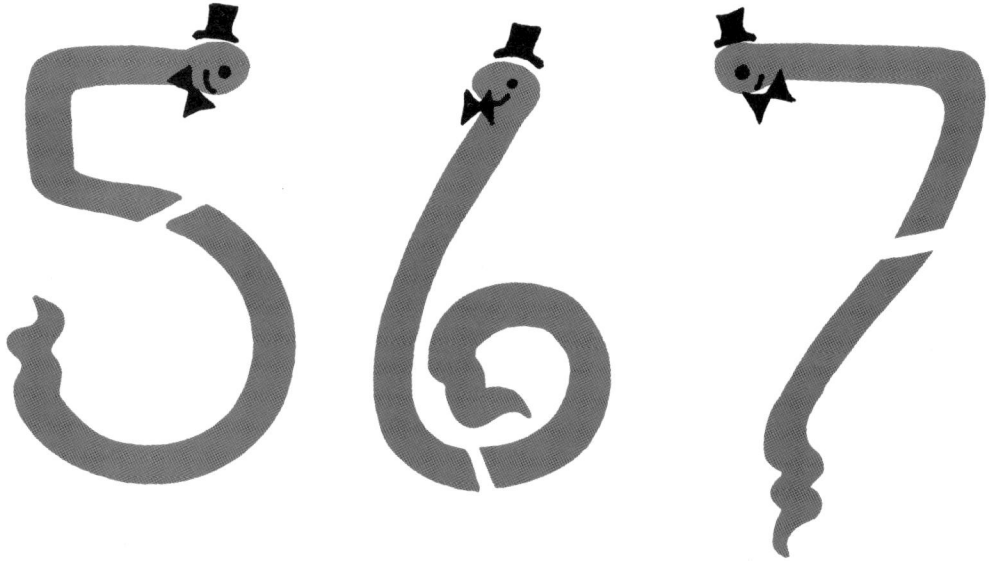